Letters on
Christian
Education

Letters on Christian Education

By A Mother

SIMPSON
PUBLISHING COMPANY

Simpson Publishing Company
Post Office Box 100
Avinger, Texas 75630

Printed in the United States of America

Library of Congress Cataloging-in-Publication Data

Mother, 19th cent.
 Letters on Christian education / by a mother.
  p.   cm.
 "The letters were originally published in the mid 1800s by
the American Tract Society under the same title . . . The
grammar, punctuation, and diction of this edition have been
revised moderately"—Pref.
 Includes bibliography
 ISBN 0-9622508-8-0
 1. Child rearing—Religious aspects—Christianity.
2. Children—Religious life.   I. Title.
BV4529.M67   1993
248.8'45—dc20

                                    93-13691
                                    CIP

Contents

Publisher's Preface

HAVE YOU EVER wanted to visit with and ask an experienced Christian parent, especially one from an older generation, "How did you do it? What were your goals? How would you cultivate the virtue of honesty? What would you do when things went wrong?" These brief but profound letters provide such an opportunity. They are the testimony of a spiritually-minded and experienced mother to a younger Christian woman. You will find in them sound biblical counsel and practical personal advice concerning the training and education of children — from infants just entering the world to teens about to leave the home and face the world on their own.

First-time and prospective parents will find these letters to be a faithful guide and introduction to what it means to raise children in the fear and admonition of the Lord. Experienced parents will be challenged by the perspectives of a generation which excelled our own in the matter of raising children according to biblical principles. Common obstacles and sins which often hinder the best of parents are identified along with their remedies. Even those acquainted with the old paths will find encouragement in these pages to persevere and pursue more earnestly the holy privilege and responsibility of raising children.

This is a book you will want to read and re-read. Each time you will be impressed with the significance of heeding the directive of Deuteronomy 6:6–7: "And these words which I command you today shall be in your heart; you shall teach them diligently to your children, and shall talk of them when you sit in your house, when you walk by the way, when you lie down, and when you rise up."

The letters were originally published in the mid-1800s by the American Tract Society under the same title. Beyond the fact that the author was a mother, having first-hand experience with the subject matter, she remains anonymous.

The grammar, punctuation, and diction of this edition have been revised moderately in order to bring the language into more conformity with contemporary usage. Titles have been added to each letter and Scripture references have been inserted where appropriate.

Letters on Christian Education

Letter 1

The Eternal Significance of Child Training

My Dear L.,

If the existence of your children were limited to a few years and then the soul and body were to expire together, maternal tenderness would impel you to make the life, which was to be so short, as happy as possible. With a mother's vigilance you would seek to render this brief period a season of uninterrupted sunshine. This temporal life, though prolonged to fourscore years, is as a stream to the ocean, when compared with eternity. Yet the unutterable interests of the soul, in that boundless immortality, are suspended upon the manner in which this fleeting moment is employed. Upon its wise improvement or abuse depends our eternal possession of joys which eye hath not seen, nor ear heard, nor the heart of man conceived, or our irrevocable doom to the prison of despair.

To train up our children for one of these abodes is the work assigned to us. My heart faints in view of the responsibility, a responsibility which we can never measure until by the light of eternity we perceive the influence of all the circumstances, associations, instructions, and events which combine to form the character of an immortal being; until our minds are sufficiently expanded to appreciate the happiness of a redeemed spirit, and the misery of a lost soul.

This responsibility calls for the highest degree of diligence, the most solicitous watchfulness, a spirit of wisdom, and fervor in prayer, which none but God can bestow. May our minds ever be awed with the consideration of the final results of duty faithfully performed or heedlessly neglected.

If you were aware of the high trust deposited in you when you received into your arms your firstborn infant, you delayed not a moment, with a heart full of gratitude, yet trembling with fear for the future, to say, "O that this child might live before Thee!" Often did you renew this petition and solemnly covenant with God in the closet. In thus dedicating your children to God, you chose Him for their Father, Jesus Christ for their Saviour, and the Holy Spirit for their Sanctifier. You chose a treasure in Heaven for their riches, the service of Christ for their employment, and the honor of being children of God as their highest distinction. You engaged, by the assistance of His grace, submissively to receive every affliction dispensed by His providence respecting them; and, if He should recall them, to say, "Thou hast taken thine own; Thy will be done." A frequent consideration of these solemn engagements will help us to sustain the loss of our children. It will excite us to fidelity. Especially will it arouse us to fervent prayer that they may begin to serve God here and in eternity, to the praise and glory of His rich grace in Christ Jesus.

Yours truly,

Letter 2

CRUCIAL ASPECTS OF
PARENTAL INSTRUCTION AND DISCIPLINE

My Dear L.,

The affectionate husband and the tender and judicious father will afford most efficient aid by the general influence of his character upon his family by his counsel, by the respect which he will manifest for the feelings and opinions of the mother of his children, and often by the direct exercise of his authority. But *early* instruction and discipline are necessarily the peculiar work of the mother. It is her steady and gentle influence, and the daily, incidental instructions which fall from her lips, that are to form the infant mind and give a direction to the character. A sensible and pious mother once remarked, "If I may have but ten years of the life of a man of seventy, to form his character, give me the first ten."

Many parents, who would on no account fail in governing their children properly, defeat their own designs in this particular: by delaying to bring them under subjection, until their wills have become obstinate, their passions strong, and until, by frequent practice, they have learned to govern, rather than to obey. This delay arises in part from the idea, as erroneous as it is prevalent, that children do not understand what is required of them until at least two years old; and in part from a secret dread of which perhaps the parent is scarcely conscious, of beginning this contest for supremacy. This is a radical error and the frequent cause of habitual disobedience and open rebellion in succeeding years. I once heard a clergyman remark that "the overbearing spirit which is exhibited in the cradle is the same which in manhood constitutes the despot and the tyrant." I would be the last to recommend the corporeal punishment of an infant; but there are few

children of eight or ten months old, who do not
sometimes attempt to procure the gratification of
their wishes by passionate crying, or obstinate perseverance. If you would have them understand at the
very outset that you are to govern, never give them
the desired object until they become quiet. Severity
of manner is unnecessary and would be unkind; you
have only to be yourself tranquil, and your child will
soon become so. You may think yourself a favored
mother, if before your little ones have attained the
age of eighteen months, you are not compelled to
subdue them by the gentle use of the rod.

At this period they are incapable of being influ-
enced by reason, and yet have sufficient intelligence
to be determined in their own way. If they are
indulged in this determination because they are too
young to be reasoned with, their resolution will soon
acquire a degree of strength which neither the force
of reason, nor the use of corporeal punishment, can
easily conquer. I know that this method is often
denounced as a remnant of unenlightened ages or of
puritanic prejudice, but Christian parents will seek to
be directed by God's word. There we are taught that

"He that spares the rod hates his son, but he that loves him, chastens him promptly" (Proverbs 13:24). I know how the parental heart shrinks from this trial. I know the conflict between tender maternal feelings and a deep conviction of duty under such circumstances. As you value the well-being of your child and your own future peace, never yield when you have once attempted to produce an obedient spirit. Lift up your heart to Him who gives power to the faint (Isaiah 40:28-31), and then go forward with quiet firmness. You will succeed; you will have the happiness of seeing the turbulent and rebellious spirit followed by gentleness and affectionate obedience.

There is a great difference in the dispositions of children. Those who are naturally gentle may never need a repetition of this mode of correction for the same offense, while others of a quick temper may oblige you to resort to it, painful as it is, again and again. Should this be the case, do not be discouraged. Prevent, whenever it is possible, the excitement of self-will. However, if self-will be excited, never yield to it. If you are careful, by steadiness and consistency, not to lose what you have gained, your children will learn to practice self-control. They will probably, in time, become habitually obedient.

Were I to attempt to enumerate the motives for thus early subduing the waywardness of children, I should find myself lost in a subject too extensive for the limits of these letters. Their happiness and usefulness, every day and hour, will greatly depend upon it. When I see devout Christians perpetually subjected to trials which originate in faults produced in them by early indulgence, and when I see the hand of God chastising them for these faults that they may be made partakers of his holiness, I cannot but say, from what severe providential correction we may save our children by seasonably subjecting them to the wholesome discipline of parental authority.

The opinions of parents on this subject should be *united*. Their government should be so perfectly blended that the will of the one shall ever be seen to be the will of the other also. Thus, when reproved or corrected by the father, the child will not expect sympathy from the mother; or if by the mother, will not think of appealing to the father. If in any instance, however small, there is a difference of views between parents with respect to the children, the mother should yield her opinion and act with the father. Afterward, in the absence of the children, she should seek union of sentiment upon the point in question. I can scarcely believe that there ever was a child who could not be made submissive to the wise decision of united parents. However, for the lack of union in opinion and practice, many a family is ruined both for this life and that which is to come; many a husband and wife are permanently alienated, and the home which might have exhibited that most lovely of all earthly scenes, a harmonious family, is converted into the abode of discord and misery.

It is expedient to make only a few rules, lest you should be frequently obliged to pass the violation of them unnoticed, or to administer reproof so often, as to harden the feelings and render admonition ineffectual. Children are incapable of retaining a great number of rules. They are heedless, and will remain so, until by observation and experience they have acquired some knowledge of what is expected of them.

It is of far greater importance than is generally supposed that the language which we employ while talking with our children should be perfectly *intelligible* to them. The waywardness of a child, who is compelled to listen to commands and expostulations which he does not understand, will inevitably become confirmed obstinacy. Conscientious and diligent parents will see their efforts for the good of their children worse than unavailing, while they themselves are the cause of the evils which perplex and distress them.

The difficulties attendant upon the government of children are great and of frequent occurrence, but the greatest of all is the difficulty of *ruling one's own spirit.* How often is a mother amidst her numerous and pressing cares, so disturbed in her feelings that, although she be not really ill-humored, she has lost that mildness of demeanor by which she was accustomed to quiet the restless spirits of her children. A recollection of the follies of our own childhood will tend to allay this impatience. A candid inspection of our hearts will convince us that we are indebted to the customs of society, the restraints of pride, or a sense of propriety or duty, for the concealment of the very faults which trouble us in our children. But believe me, my dear friend, nothing will act so powerfully and produce so wholesome an effect upon your little ones, even when they are not more than two or three years old, as that self-possession on your part which is the result of communion with God. When you find yourself assailed by a thousand perplexities and annoyed with the follies of your children, so that you are tempted to speak unadvisedly with your lips, fly to the closet and implore the ornament of a meek and quiet spirit (1 Peter 3:4) and the patience and gentleness of Christ. If you do not immediately obtain that tranquility which you seek, go again and again. God hears prayer, and blessed be His name, He gives wisdom liberally without reproach to them that ask Him (James 1:5). Go then to Him and you will learn by sweet experience that the soul which is filled with spiritual peace can quietly endure the little adversities of life.

Yours truly,

Letter 3

Cultivating Honesty and Justice

My Dear L.,

Should you early succeed in training your children to habits of "prompt and cheerful obedience," you will still find that many evils remain to be vanquished. It is a humiliating truth that our children possess a fallen nature, and with this we have to contend at every step in their education. While they are greatly endeared to us by their winning ways and lovely traits of character, we are painfully compelled to see that they early "go astray" from God "speaking lies" (Psalm 58:3).

Probably there are few parents who have escaped the agony of knowing for the first time that a beloved child has uttered a deliberate falsehood. The disposition to deceive exhibits itself in a variety of forms in young children; and it should be carefully watched and steadily resisted. It is indispensable to the formation of upright and trustworthy character that every disingenuous, artful habit should be prevented or eradicated. So far as you can with safety, confide in their veracity. Let them see that you honor uprightness and truth and despise deceit and cunning. Our example should be blameless in this respect, for children are frequently led into the practice of deception by the lack of sincerity and integrity in those about them. These little creatures early learn to imitate the ways of others; with surprising vigilance and accuracy they detect inconsistencies between language and conduct. If they witness a disposition to concealment in those with whom they associate, how can it be expected that they should speak and act with frankness? But how often do we see a mother exciting the sympathy of her child by professing to be grieved and to weep!

How often too, is the little whippersnapper bribed into giving an unwilling greeting, by the promise of seeing the horse or the birds or some other object, which it was not intended should be shown him. Unpardonable indiscretion!

It is to be feared that children are often driven to making false representations in their own favor by the exercise of too great severity toward their faults. Here is a motive, could none be derived from the tender regard due to their feelings, to induce us to avoid a harsh course of conduct toward them. The child who resorts to artful subterfuges, and fears to tell the truth lest he should meet with unkind treatment, is indeed to be pitied. I am reminded by these thoughts of a sentiment expressed by the excellent Cotton Mather in his *Essay Upon the Duties of Parents*: "The slavish, boisterous manner of governing children, too commonly used, I consider as no small article in the wrath and curse of God upon a miserable world." Be careful then, when your children are in fault, especially if you suppose yourself wholly or in part unacquainted with the circumstances, to encourage them by your mildness to tell you the whole affair: bidding them recollect exactly how it took place. Remind them that God, who knows all things, will know whether they speak truthfully and will be greatly displeased if they speak falsely. If after all your care the child will not acknowledge the truth, parental fidelity requires you to punish him; and, as I think, with the rod, for such is the manner in which this sin is spoken of in the Bible. So woeful are the effects of its indulgence, that I cannot see how Christian parents can acquit themselves before God and their own conscience without showing toward it severe displeasure.

Let your conduct on these occasions be such as to make a deep impression upon the heart of your child. Take him immediately into a private, secluded room. With affectionate solemnity tell him the dreadful nature of the sin which he has committed. Repeat to him those passages of Scripture in which God has expressed his displeasure against the sin of lying. Read to him the story of Ananias and Sapphira. Ask him earnestly if he wishes to be happy here and to go and live with God and all the good in heaven; to repent and beg God to forgive him, and keep him from doing so any more. After this pray with him, carefully adapting your petitions to his case and your language to his understanding. Possibly the solemnity of these instructions and admonitions may produce that tender contrition and abhorrence of his crime which will furnish a high degree of assurance that it will not be repeated. If so, and if this be the first offense of the kind, it will be safe to omit the use of more severe means. Otherwise tell him that God in the Bible requires you to punish him for such sins, and that you must obey. After having administered the chastisement, more painful no doubt to you than to him, induce him to kneel down and in his own language ask the forgiveness of his heavenly Father. I have seen the powerful influence of this method in producing uprightness and integrity of character. God blesses His own word; and if we more frequently availed ourselves of its authority and of the influence of prayer upon our little ones, we should be happier parents, and they would be better and happier children.

Intimately connected with this subject is the cultivation of a sense of justice. Opportunities daily occur in a family with young children for teaching them the obligations of justice; and no pains should be spared, and no suitable occasion omitted, to enforce upon them the respect due to each other's rights. The snatching of a plaything from its owner ought never to be winked at or overlooked. The offender should not only be reminded of the impropriety of his conduct, but of the sin of taking from another that which is not his. They should also be made to feel that they have no right to play with or to use each other's toys without the consent of the owner. Lest you should by example counteract the influence of precept, always restore to a child that of which you may have deprived him by way of correction.

Our Saviour's golden rule will be understood by children almost as soon as they are capable of teasing each other in the manner described above. After they have learned to repeat it, it is surprising with what facility they will apply it to their own conduct and that of others. I once heard a little girl of four and a half years, while playing with her younger brother, say to him, "Shall I tell you the meaning of the golden rule?" She then repeated it and said, "This means that I must be just as kind and obliging to you as I should like to have you be to me. Do you understand what is meant by doing good to them that hate you?" He replied, "No." "Then I will tell you. If any one is very, very unkind to you, you must be very kind to him. Do you understand now?" "Yes," was the answer. Condescending Saviour, I thank you that so many of thy holy precepts are adapted to the understanding of a little child!

Yours,

Letter 4

Cultivating Honorable Speech and Courtesy

My Dear L.,

There is one error in practice from which I fear but few parents are wholly exempt. It is the indulgence of severe remarks upon the faults and weaknesses of others. If evil speaking were not classed in the Bible with the most heinous offenses, an application of that infallible test, the golden rule, would reveal its true nature. It brings with it a train of evils, and its effects are most unhappy upon the manners, and what is far worse, upon the heart. Never allow your children to amuse themselves at the expense of others; nor unnecessarily expose to their view the faults of your acquaintances. Especially avoid making unkind remarks about the character or performances of your minister. The consequences of slander, or even of criticism in this case, may be such as you will bitterly lament when it is too late to obtain a remedy.

The utmost vigilance is insufficient with most families to shield children entirely from the influence of vicious example. This is particularly the case in large towns where they can scarcely walk the length of a street without hearing profane language. There are few children thus exposed who do not at some time transgress the third commandment. If there can be a sin more to be dreaded than lying, it is this. If you would not see your children abandoned as despisers of God and of every thing sacred, meet their first approaches to it with marked displeasure, accompanied with a clear explanation of the nature of the crime and solemn admonitions against the repetition of it. Should this prove insufficient to check the evil, your duty and the well-being of your child require that you punish him with severity.

The habitual use of mild and suitable language is highly important. Vulgarity stands next to vice in its disastrous influence upon children and youth. If profaneness and licentiousness are to be dreaded, see that the way for their entrance be not prepared by the use of expressions and the indulgence of manners which are an offense against delicacy and propriety.

You will have it in your power to promote in your children the early exercise of kind and gentle feelings. Appropriate occasions will occur daily for inculcating this part of their duty. But in this respect, as in all others, "a mother should *be* what she wishes her children to *become*." *Example* is the most efficient kind of instruction. You will then perceive the importance of daily exhibiting that amiableness and affection, that interest for the happiness and attention to the wants of others, by which life is so much sweetened and the human character so greatly improved. How is it possible that our children should be adorned with lovely traits of character and amiable manners, if they are accustomed to have their tender expressions and childish kindnesses coldly received or disregarded?

Children should be taught to be attentive to the feelings and convenience of others. Let it not be thought that politeness is necessary only in grown people or among the fashionable. The amiable Doddridge calls the forms of politeness "the outworks of humanity." The Earl of Chatham, in his *Letters to His Nephew*, defines politeness as "benevolence in trifles." The apostle Peter instructed the Christians to whom he wrote to "be courteous" (1 Peter 3:8). The apostle Paul, among other directions to the Romans, exhorts them "in honor" to "prefer one another" (Romans 12:10).

The practice of neatness and regularity is also of great consequence. The brightest virtues may be obscured and the usefulness of the most devout may be hindered by the want of good habits in these respects. Many conscientious people seem to regard these as but *little things*. I answer, it is the combination of a thousand little circumstances which forms the character and gives direction to the whole life. Look at two families exhibiting opposite examples in these respects. Which has the fairest prospect of being brought under the influence of religion and

which promises to be most useful in the community?
No, there are no trifles in the work of education.

Yours,

Letter 5

IMPARTING THE KNOWLEDGE OF GOD

My Dear L.

If we are true Christians our first wish for our children will be that they may early be brought into the fold of the great Shepherd, and thus be shielded from those enemies of the soul by which so many youths are fatally enticed. Oh, if there is any thing which should constrain us at early dawn, when surrounded with midday cares, at evening hour, yes, and in the watches of the night, to enter into the closet; if there is any thing which should lead us to God with a fervor of supplication surpassing that with which we plead for our own souls, it is the early conversion of our children!

We have the example of Timothy, of St. Augustine, and in later times of Hooker, Doddridge, Wesley, Newton, Dwight and many others, to illustrate the blessed effects of maternal faithfulness. Could the history of the most pious of every age be exposed to our view, I cannot doubt we should see that to the instrumentality of a mother's teaching, the world is indebted for its greatest benefactors and the church for her most illustrious sons.

One of the most delightful offices of a mother is that of leading the minds of her little children up to God as a Father. Early they should be taught that He takes care of them every day and keeps them safely every night; that He knows when they are sick and pities them; that it is He that cures them and gives them kind parents to love and watch over them. They should be taught short prayers such as they will perfectly understand; they should be encouraged to offer some one of them morning and evening. And often at these times the heart of the devout mother will be gladdened by the intelligent inquiries of the little children about the great God. When they have reached the age for learning these simple prayers, a new and efficient means is put into the hands of parents for influencing them to a right course of conduct. The often-repeated sentiment that God loves the good and is displeased with the wicked will make an impression upon their teachable minds. Improve the opportunity when they have been guilty of misconduct to tell them that they have a wicked heart and never will be really good until they have a new one. They should be persuaded to go alone and confess their sin and ask their heavenly Father to make them better. The frequent referral of their sins and troubles to God will powerfully tend to teach them that happiness is inseparable from love and obedience to God. It will make them feel the importance of prayer and prepare them to understand their need of a Saviour.

I know of no way in which we can so effectually impart to children a knowledge of God and their duty, as by instructing them in the history and precepts of the Bible. A new era in the religious condition of mankind will commence when parents universally seek to govern their children by the influence of the Bible and to form their opinions upon the principles which it inculcates. This is not to be done by occasional or stated exhortations upon the subject of religion. The morality of the Bible must be applied to their daily conduct. By this unerring standard we must habitually teach them to judge their feelings and behavior. The remarks which have been made respecting the golden rule will apply with equal force to a great number of Scriptural precepts. I have seen the petulance of a little child instantly checked by being reminded of this text: "Be kind one to another, tender-hearted, forgiving one another, even as God, for Christ's sake, forgives you."

Almost the first wish expressed by a little one after he can speak intelligibly is to hear a story; and with none are children so delighted as with those narrations which abound in the Scriptures. We should avail ourselves of this desire to pour divine knowledge into their tender minds and thus open to them the fountain of religious truth. If we perform this duty with fidelity, we shall be abundantly repaid at every step not only in the pleasure with which we shall be heard but also in the benefit derived to our own minds.

The story of Moses, concealed by his anxious mother by the side of the river, exposed to be devoured by crocodiles, discovered and adopted by the King's daughter, and nursed by his own mother, will awaken deep interest. After they have become familiar with these circumstances, tell them of his progress in learning, and that he became a pious man, and that God employed him to do a great deal of good. Perhaps they will inquire, "Where is he now?" And when you have told them that he is in heaven and that all good people will go there, it will be well to add that if they love and obey their heavenly Father they will go there too. God's displeasure with the wicked and His kind care of the good may be illustrated by the history of the deluge and in the inimitable story of Joseph and his brethren. The sad effects of anger and ill will may be strikingly exhibited by the story of Cain and Abel. The manner in which one sin leads to another should be pointed out in Cain's answer, when God questioned him concerning his brother.

It is very important to communicate these histories in a *gradual* manner, making them perfectly familiar with one story before you relate to them another. Carefully observe also whether you are understood by your little auditors. The pains taken by many parents to instruct their children are often lost because they do not understand the meaning of the words which are used. If they appear listless and inattentive, we may be sure (unless they are fatigued by prolonged attention) that our language is above their comprehension. This error, if continued, will not only defeat our object in teaching them, but give them a distaste for religious instruction, by which we shall be deprived of the means of access to their minds and thus of the opportunity of doing them good.

When they are old enough to learn the commandments they will be filled with wonder and a salutary awe on hearing of the manner in which they were given on Mount Sinai. They will express their surprise that these are the same commandments which they are taught. They will eagerly inquire whether Moses, who saw and talked with the great God, is the same that was laid in the ark of bulrushes by the side of the river.

The story of Samuel is one which invariably delights a child. Relate it minutely, and point out the condescension of our heavenly Father in speaking to a little boy. On some occasion when you are obliged to correct them, tell them of the troubles which were sent upon Eli and his sons because of his unfaithfulness to them and their disobedience to him. Then tell them that you will displease God by indulging their misconduct. Tell them of Daniel's courageous perseverance in the service of God and his preservation from the fury of the lions. And here again, the love and care of our gracious Father toward such as obey and trust Him may be happily impressed upon their minds. The sad consequences of disobedience to God cannot be more vividly portrayed than in the history of Jonah.

It would be unnecessary to mention all the Scripture narrations in which most valuable instruction and entertainment are mingled, and by which the minds of children may be enriched with divine knowledge. Indeed, when I consider the inexhaustible sources of instruction contained in the Bible, and the appropriateness of its diversified examples and holy precepts to young minds, I am surprised that we should ever be at a loss of how to entertain and teach our children.

It is of infinite importance that your children have just views of our blessed Saviour. The happiest consequences may result from a proper exhibition of His character and works and a judicious inculcation of His instructions. Let me say to you that you will never communicate the knowledge of Him so suitably and with such happy effect as when your own soul is filled with His Spirit. Learn of Him who was meek and lowly in heart and whose meat and drink it was to do the will of His Father, and you can scarcely fail to produce in your children reverence for His character and respect for His precepts. Endeavor to impress them deeply with a sense of His wonderful condescension and love, in laying aside the glory which He had with the Father before the world was, and assuming our nature, that we might be redeemed from eternal destruction. Make them acquainted with His history from His humble birth through His life of sorrows, His crucifixion, resurrection, and ascension into heaven. Tell them of the miracles which He wrought, His continual acts of benevolence, His tender sympathy for the afflicted, His condescension to little children, His forbearance toward the wicked, His forgiveness of His enemies, and His meek endurance of suffering in the garden and on the cross. Mingle your instructions with remarks upon the odious nature of sin which was the cause of all this humiliation and suffering. Seek to make them understand the necessity of repentance, of love to Christ, and of trust in Him in order to being saved. When you observe them tenderly affected by what they have heard from you, pray with them, minutely confessing their faults, and affectionately commending them to the mercy of this kind Saviour.

This method of instruction has been found to be exceedingly happy in giving just views of God and our obligations to him and in producing a general improvement which it is difficult to describe, unless it be called a moral cultivation of the whole character. In this way their consciences are enlightened and made tender to such a degree that it would seem impossible they should ever be so far lost to a sense of moral obligation as to become confirmed in vice. They may indeed for a while be entangled and beguiled by the fascinations of a wicked world. But, even in the haunts of sin, which are as the suburbs of hell, the conscience once enlightened will thunder its remonstrances in the pale delinquent's ear and remind him of the prayers and exhortations of a pious father and mother. Thus will early instructions "hang upon the wheels of evil," and at this dark hour it may be that the wanderer will arise with a penitent heart and go to his heavenly Father.

It may be thought that I do not sufficiently recognize the work of the Holy Spirit in sanctifying the heart and that too much efficacy is attributed to religious instruction. I answer that we do not look for the rewards of industry without its toils, nor the autumn harvest without having cast in the seed and cultivated the soil. We are taught in the Scriptures that the Holy Spirit does not commonly sanctify men without means; and that this is the way in which we are to expect a blessing upon our offspring. Moses in speaking to the Israelites of the manner in which they should inculcate the precepts of religion says, "And you shall teach them diligently unto your children, and shall talk of them, when you sit in your house, and when you walk by the way, and when you lie down, and when you rise up" (Deuteronomy 6:7). Of Timothy it is said that "from a child [he] had known the Holy Scriptures, which were able to make [him] wise unto salvation, through faith in Christ Jesus" (2 Timothy 3:15). Our Saviour prayed that his disciples might be sanctified "through the truth" (John 17:17). We have the highest possible encouragement to pursue this course because God declares that He will bless His own word; and we see that He does so. Who can tell but, in some favored hour, the Holy Spirit may descend and fill the hearts of our children with the love of God through the instrumentality of those instructions which are derived from the Bible. Let us then take courage; let us with diligence, patience, and love pour these divine truths into their minds and never cease to implore God's blessing, without which all our efforts will be fruitless.

Yours,

Letter 6

OBSERVING THE SABBATH WITH WISDOM

My Dear L.,

The manner in which the Sabbath should be spent is a subject of too much consequence to be passed over in silence. All parents, doubtless, encounter many difficulties in leading their children to a proper observance of the sacred day; and my own embarrassments on this subject will lead me to offer my advice with diffidence.

It is not to be supposed that any one can interest children in religious duties so deeply as their parents. Their influence to restrain them from improprieties

will be greater than that of any other. You will therefore find it necessary to devote nearly your whole
time on the Sabbath to your little family with the
exception of the hours of private devotion and public
worship.

The Sabbath and every thing connected with the
subject of religion should be rendered pleasant if
possible. Many truly pious people increase to a high
degree the natural aversion of their children to divine
things by the severity with which they administer
instruction. Contempt of religion, hardness of heart,
and infidelity itself are the frequent consequences of
often-repeated, reproachful, overbearing admonition.

Is there not, however, at the present day a fearful
absence of that high reverence for the Sabbath which
characterized the days of our fathers? If it be not kept
as a day in which we must neither "think our own
thoughts, speak our own words, nor find our own
pleasures" (Isaiah 58:13), disrespect for divine ordi-
nances and instructions will ensue. The children thus
brought up will be advocates for those customs in
the community which tend to remove the landmarks

of religion. Our deportment on the Lord's Day should be such as to discountenance all trifling conversation and unnecessary secular employment, and to impress the minds of our families with the conviction that this is a season which is solemnly set apart for the sacred duties.

The telling of Scripture stories as before described may be practiced with excellent effect upon the Sabbath. You will derive much assistance from a Bible or sacred history with illustrations. These will be particularly useful in the instruction of the little ones who have not learned to read. With respect to the older children, instead of giving them a long lesson for the occupation of the whole day, let their employments be varied. Require them to study a portion of Bible history and relate it in their own language; or, if you can obtain a book of Scripture questions, assign them one or two chapters at a lesson. These catechisms generally awaken interest and cannot be recited without an accurate knowledge of the parts of Scripture to which they relate. You will derive great assistance from sharing in their employments and studies. Their interest in reading will be increased by your reading with them. If you yourself learn a hymn or catechetical lesson to recite with them, they will be the more solicitous to learn theirs well.

Children who are old enough to write should be furnished with a blank book and be required to remember the texts and leading thoughts of the sermons which they hear, and to write them after their return from worship. This practice is productive of at least three good effects: it furnishes one method of employing the time suitably on the Sabbath; the frequent expression of the thoughts of others in their own language will give them facility in conversation and writing; and a habit of attention to preaching will also be created, which is of immense consequence. How often is the faithful minister grieved with the conviction that his toils in the study have availed nothing for the good of his people, because they have not listened to his instructions in the sanctuary. How many hearts remain unaffected by religious truth because its language does not enter the ear?

It is one of the pleasant characteristics of the present period that those juvenile books and memoirs of pious children, which were once rarely to be found, may be obtained in every village. A well regulated taste for these books will be very beneficial; and much assistance may be derived from the use of them, particularly for those who have passed the period of childhood.

As the Sabbath draws toward a close, the father and mother should accompany their children to a retired room. After hearing their recitations and tenderly counseling them, as their characters require, the parents should fervently give them up in prayer to that God, who keeps covenant and shows mercy, that they may be his children for ever. The half hour thus spent will be a hallowed season to devout parents. If their own hearts are made tender by the holy influence of religious duties, the minds of their children will receive a salutary impression.

You must expect to meet with discouragements, and sometimes to witness the entire failure of every endeavor to make your children spend the day properly; but a correct example, and unwearied diligence, it may be hoped, will at length accomplish

the end which you seek — their reverential observance of the Sabbath.

Yours,

Letter 7

CULTIVATING BENEVOLENCE AND SELF-DENIAL

My Dear L.,

Parents at the present day are under peculiar obligations to train their children into the benevolent spirit of the age. Having steadily endeavored to pursue such a course in their education as shall prepare them for the service of Christ, we must remember that this is a period of the world in which the great Head of the Church is pleased in a special manner to honor His people by making them co-workers with Him in the cause of truth and righteousness. We should earnestly seek for our children the exalted privilege of being thus employed.

If our supplications to God for them, that they may be *wholly* his, are *sincere*, the supplications will also be *unconditional*. When we are permitted to make near approaches to our heavenly Father, we should there in His presence ask ourselves whether we are willing that he should call them to privation, suffering, or death itself, for the advancement of His kingdom. Remembering our weakness, let us plead that when He puts our fidelity to the trial, He will not permit us to break our commitments.

Too long have Christians sought worldly ease for themselves and their children. It is a low and ignoble course for those who profess to love a crucified Saviour and the souls which he died to redeem. We *must* seek to have our children eminently instrumental in alleviating the temporal miseries of this wretched world and of saving immortal beings from the wrath to come. What honor could be so high! What pursuit so ennobling! What course so safe! How does the contemplation of this glorious work cast into insignificance the trifling pursuits and ephemeral pleasures of the merry worldling! Let the hearts of our children glow with an inextinguishable desire to do good. Let us see them treading in the steps of Howard, Martyn, Mills, and Hall, and we will ask no more.

We should early and uniformly endeavor to make them sensible of their high obligations to live for the glory of God and the good of their fellow men. We should inculcate the duty of habitual self-denial and endeavor to influence them to the practice of it in the hope of being useful. Our example should convince them that the great business of our lives is to do good and that we shrink from no sacrifice or exertion for this purpose. Let their sympathies be early awakened for the friendless and homeless. When enjoying their comfortable meals and soft beds, remind them of the poor children who suffer with hunger and nakedness and have not where to lay their heads. Inform them of the miserable situation of those who never heard of the true God and who worship idols of wood and stone. Point out to them the sad effects of heathenism in destroying parental affection and filial respect and obedience in bringing upon both parents and children the greatest miseries of this life, and in sinking them into eternal perdition. They will not need to be *compelled* to reserve a part of their spending money and to make other sacrifices that they may aid in sending them Bibles and teachers. The sympathies of children are easily excited. Thus, the Creator has put into our hands the most pleasing facilities for influencing them to acts of kindness toward the miserable and unhappy.

But without the renewing and sanctifying influences of the Holy Spirit, benevolence will not be an inwrought principle of the character; self-denial will not be uniformly practiced. Every day, then, should witness our increased solicitude and our more earnest prayers that the hearts of our children may be filled with the love of God now, so that their whole lives may be employed in doing good.

Yours,

Letter 8

My Dear L.,

A lack of success in the education of children may frequently be traced to one of the following errors: the neglect to establish a habit of subordination; the unsteady and inconsistent exercise of authority; extreme severity; or the lack of parental unity. The same evil consequences, though in different proportions, will commonly arise from each. If we fall into any, we must not be surprised to find ourselves involved in perplexity, and distressed with apprehensions, when our children attain to the period of youth. Our

daughters will be vain, deceitful, selfish, and disre-
spectful. Our sons will be obstinate, self-sufficient,
and probably vicious. It will be too late to retrace the
steps by which this sad result was accomplished. Rigid
restraint will confirm an obstinate child. It will
exasperate one with an irritable temper and rouse a
spirit of rebellion which will defy parental influence
and filial obligation. All that we can do in such a case
is to watch with unsleeping vigilance and love for
every opportunity of imparting instruction, adminis-
tering caution, fleeing from temptation, encouraging
industry, winning confidence and affection, and
making home attractive. Possibly these late efforts
may avert the worst evils resulting from such errors as
have been mentioned, but regenerating grace is the
only effectual remedy. The Spirit of God can bring
their hearts into the obedience of Christ and establish
in them the living principle of every virtue.

But if a proper course has been pursued in childhood, we may hope that parental control will be
maintained in youth without the use of coercive
measures or the exercise of absolute authority. The
influence of wise instructions, reasonable requests

and consistent conduct, accompanied by "a constant flow of love that knows no fall," will prepare them for a gradual change from the *authority* of the parent to the influence of a *superior friend*. Genuine religion excepted, parental friendship will more effectively guard young people from going astray than all other influences combined. The desire of gratifying the wishes and receiving the approbation of beloved and revered parents, whose happiness is interwoven with his own well-being, will be to a well-educated youth a powerful restraint from vice and a strong incentive to good conduct. Let then the interests of your children be identified as closely as possible with those of their parents. Seek to possess their entire confidence, so that when they do wrong, they will be the first to tell you of it. Encourage them freely to make known their feelings, opinions, pleasures, and sorrows to you. Never let your sons feel that their father will frown upon these communications as too trifling to deserve his attention, or that their mother will hear them with indifference. Habitually endeavor to make them happy in your society and to fasten their attachment to home. One of the best methods of accomplishing this desirable end is regarded too little by parents generally; it is the habit of conversing with their children upon useful and interesting subjects. Knowledge promotes happiness; and how can it be so pleasantly conveyed as by the lips of an intelligent, affectionate father and mother? Those parents who feel themselves deficient in mental cultivation would be amply repaid for exerting themselves and acquiring knowledge by the benefits which the communication would have upon their children's characters.

A frequent cause of failure in education is that a *habit of industry* is not seasonably and firmly established. It has been justly remarked that industry is the fountain under God of all human attainments and enjoyments. Without it the most splendid talents are comparatively useless; with it an ordinary mind may rise to high attainment and extensive usefulness. Those men who have been most distinguished in politics, literature, science, or any branch of knowledge owe their elevation and usefulness in a great measure to the regular distribution and diligent improvement of time. Industry is as essential to the respectability and happiness of the rich as of the poor. Idleness is as fatal to the well-being of the heir of a millionaire as to the child of a day-laborer. There is not a single immortal being whose wealth can purchase for him the right to be wasteful of time. Idleness not only prevents the future usefulness and happiness of children but also makes them an easy prey to temptation, leads them to kill time in evil company, and is the prolific parent of the worst vices.

If it is necessary that our sons be removed from home for a public education, or for the acquiring of a knowledge of active business, it is obviously important that we place them where wholesome restraint is exerted and a steady moral influence felt. We should commit them to the instruction or superintendence of those who daily discharge every duty in the fear and love of God; and we should endeavor to secure for them the friendship of religious associates. In thus placing them beyond our immediate oversight and committing them to the direction of others, care must be taken that our influence over them not be lost. They should, therefore, be frequently visited by their parents and especially by their father. Both parents should often address letters to them which show concern for their happiness, counsel them against temptation, and remind them of their high obligations to God and to the Saviour who died that sinners might live.

There may be instances of children who sustain little injury from promiscuous dealings with vicious companions. However, the opinion that as they are to live in the world they should early be made familiar with a view of its corruptions is, with rare exceptions, a destructive one in practice. Our own resolution is not proof against temptation. Nothing is more commonly remarked by us than our need of divine restraints from sin. Shall then the pliant young mind be exposed to the influence of evil example? No youth should be left to the exercise of his own discretion in the choice of companions until good habits have become fixed and his mind so deeply impressed with an abhorrence of vice that he will choose to associate only with youth of good principles and correct deportment. Especially should he be excluded from the society of those who ridicule religion and religious people. What evil cannot this one weapon accomplish! How often has it swept away from young minds all reverence for sacred things and with it the dearest parental hopes.

In conducting the education of our daughters during this period, we should be directed by the same general principles which apply to the guidance of our sons. As the supervision of the latter in youth is appropriately the work of the father, so the care of the former is the peculiar duty of the mother. But in well-disciplined and well-instructed families, the power of both parents over the minds of sons and daughters will be more perfect at this time than at any preceding period. What earthly scene presents such moral beauty as a family in which united parental influence and filial reverence and love are seen in perfection?

The most prominent requisites of the female character are amiableness, discretion, intelligence, and piety. These include a "family of virtues" and may be considered the cornerstones of a fair and well-proportioned edifice. A truly *Christian* mother will not be ambitious to see her daughters become fine ladies, but good children, good sisters, and good wives and mothers. With your views of human responsibility, you will consider it no trifling concern to prepare them for the duties of either of these relations, especially the last. Remember then, that the Christian character of your children's children for many generations may depend upon your wisdom and fidelity.

The endearing confidence of a judicious and godly mother is of inestimable value to young females. For the lack of it, many an amiable girl has cheered herself with the friendship of those whose influence upon her character has been most unhappy. Secure and reciprocate the confidence of your daughters, and your power over their minds will be greater than that of any other human being. Use this power to inspire them with a love for the innocent recreations, the useful and rational employments of home. Guard them against every tendency to frivolity, self-display, and excessive love of dress. These follies are too commonly cultivated, rather than repressed at this age. Many religious mothers seem to consider them as the necessary attendants of the early youth of females. Teach them to depend upon their own invention and resources for entertainment. Their buoyant spirits will be animated by every pleasant object. Every change of circumstance and season will afford enjoyment and the simplest recreations will fill them with delight. Many of the amusements which are fashionable for little girls are directly calculated to destroy all relish for these innocent, healthy, and appropriate pleasures. These amusements should be firmly discountenanced by religious people as being preparatory to extravagant dissipation at a later period. It is indeed surprising that at the age when we should expect the concern of religious parents for the conversion of their children to become intense, and their intercessions for them doubly importunate, they are often seen (as if forgetful of the infinite blessings to be won or lost) freely surrendering them to the influence of the opinions and customs of the world and aiding in their conformity to it. Does not this fact furnish an answer to the often repeated question, "Why do the children of religious people so frequently become those devoted to pleasure?" It is said of Dr. Thomas Scott, who was eminently successful in the education of his children, that "the grand secret of his success appears to have been this: that he always sought for his children, as well as for himself, in the first place, 'the kingdom of God and His righteousness.'" In his view, "this should extend, not only to the instructions directly given and the prayers offered on behalf of his family, but to his whole conduct respecting them; to the spirit and behavior habitually exhibited before them; to the value practically and evidently set upon eternal in preference to temporal things; and very particularly to the disposal of them in life; the places of instruction to which they should be sent; the families which they should visit; the connections which they should form; and the openings which should be embraced or rejected for them."

That mental cultivation which is the result of a taste for reading is, generally speaking, more necessary to the usefulness and respectability of women than of men. Numerous opportunities for observation are presented to the latter by their intercourse with the world; and those who are publicly educated are, of course, more conversant with books than females are who, after passing a few years at school, are generally from the nature of their occupations prevented from continuing the systematic cultivation of their minds. It is too commonly the case that parents congratulate themselves upon the entire discharge of their duty in reference to the mental improvement of their daughters' minds, when they have given them a good school education. Important as this is, it is not all that is requisite for the cultivation of the mind. She who, with circumscribed opportunities of attending school, devotes her leisure moments and the hours which can be spared from other duties to the reading of useful books, will acquire more information and possess more practical knowledge than the best taught female who has no taste for solid reading.

One of the most intelligent and lovely women that ever adorned society was deprived of going to school when a child, in consequence of the prejudices existing against her father's political opinions. This circumstance compelled her to depend upon her own efforts and such occasional instruction as could be given her by a mother and sisters who were suffering bitterly under the calamities of war. When relating these facts to a friend she said that she was never but once so unhappy that she could not be consoled by a book; and added, "The Spectator educated me."

A knowledge of domestic duties is an essential part of the education of females. Whether their station requires their actual labor or not, they should understand the economical, neat, and regular arrangement of household concerns. If they ever become wives, the good order and peace of their families will greatly depend upon their skilful and considerate superintendence. I will not affirm that this humble branch of knowledge is generally under-valued; but is there not danger that an exclusive appropriation of the years of early youth to study may prevent our daughters from being sufficiently interested in these employments ever to give them due attention? A lady may be very sensible, very accomplished, very elegant, and very religious; but if she is ignorant of her appropriate duties, she hazards the happiness and usefulness of herself and of her family.

Yours,

Letter 9

The Place of Entertainment and Leisure

My Dear L.,

After having bestowed unceasing attention upon the early education of your children, you may be in danger of losing the rewards of your labors in consequence of a desire to have them admired and loved by the world. Even Christians are too prone to forget the high purposes for which an immortal should live. The specious desire that their children should avoid singularity and instead should mingle with the fashionable, in order that they may exert a useful influence, is the rock upon which the hopes of many a pious parent have been dashed. And we are all in danger of being misled by the belief that *our* children have too much correct principle to become "lovers of pleasure."

The prevalent opinion that in withdrawing young people from gay amusements we deprive them of that to which their age entitles them, finds too many advocates among professors of religion. There is great justice in the remark of a late practical writer (Rev. J. James), that "young people stand in much less need, than is generally supposed, of any amusement, properly so called. Their cares are light, their sorrows few, and their occupations rarely very fatiguing to the mind." Allowing, however, that amusements are essential to the happiness of our children, we are bound to select for them such, and only such, as are innocent; and those cannot be so, which drown reflection, corrupt the morals, or impair the health.

If the pleasures of the theater will bear to be judged by this rule, let them be enjoyed. But who will say that the virtue of young people is not endangered when they enter the place which is, almost beyond all others, the nursery of vice in every form; where even if the temple were pure, the vestibule is a scene of pollution, through which a youth can scarcely pass uncontaminated. No truly modest female can witness dramatic exhibitions, as they are commonly conducted, without blushing. Shall we trust our daughters in scenes where they cannot be happy, until they lose that delicacy which is their brightest ornament? What will be the consequence to our sons of resorting to a place where the modesty of their sisters would be offended or endangered? Is this amusement favorable to their health? Is the body invigorated and the mind relaxed by loss of sleep and the agitation of excited feeling? The strongest advocates of the stage hesitate to avow that its exhibitions are actually beneficial; they only affirm that they are capable of being made so.

Let us now inquire into the benefits to be derived from the Assembly-room [a place for socializing and dancing]. Is its conversation adapted to improve the mind? Do its civilities flow from the heart and promote social kindness and valuable friendship? Are the hours chosen for resorting there more favorable to health than those of the theater? Is not the style of dress usually adopted such as to excite, rather than allay, that vanity which is so inconsistent with the humility and decorum of the Gospel? Does it not compel the wearer to expend more money, thought, and time in preparation, than can possibly be justified in a being who is hastening to the grave and to the judgment? Is it not the direct tendency of this amusement to drown reflection, to heat the imagination, to unfit the soul for holy devotion, and to produce a habit of mind totally diverse from the spirit of the Bible? Christian parents often quiet their consciences while they indulge their children in this gay pleasure by saying that genteel manners can be acquired no where but in the Dancing-school and the Assembly-room. Is it indeed so? For me, I am well convinced, that *there is more real good breeding and true politeness out of the ballroom, than is found in it.* But suppose that the assertion were true, we are admonished in God's word, "not to be conformed to this world" (Romans 12:2). Upon us rests the momentous responsibility, relying upon the aid of Divine Grace, of training them up for the holy employments and society of heaven. But is not the style of manners generally acquired there greatly deficient in gentleness, benignity, and delicacy? It is indeed wonderful that sensible parents, pious or not, can consent to exchange these inestimable graces for the forwardness and vanity of a fashionable trifler. The mind, which is cultivated by an acquaintance with books and intercourse with intelligent and refined society, and the heart that is elevated by the influence of religion, can scarcely fail of being accompanied by a propriety and ease of deportment incomparably superior to the ceremonious politeness taught by a master.

An acquaintance with music and drawing, where the circumstances of parents admit of their acquisition, will furnish recreation which is useful, independent, and ever at hand. It is desirable that a native taste for either of these arts should be cultivated to afford innocent enjoyment and produce a happy effect upon the mind. A love of the beautiful and sublime scenes in nature is a source of elevated pleasure, and may be enjoyed even from early childhood and in every station in life. Young people who have a taste for reading can scarcely be at a loss for relaxation. An interesting book will raise a depressed spirit, relieve the mind fatigued with business, and pleasantly employ the hour that would otherwise have passed heavily. The endearments of home will afford the purest happiness to young people who have been judiciously educated. Let then the domestic fire-side ever be a scene of rational enjoyment, intellectual improvement, and an affectionate interchange of kind offices between parents and children, brothers and sisters. Above all, let a dignified consistency ever be witnessed between your instructions and your practice. Let them never hear you mention the opinion of the world as the ruling motive to any course of conduct. Daily leave this testimony in their consciences, *that you seek to please God.*

Those unhappy parents whose children have become despisers of the sacred obligations of religion may tell you that early instruction and parental influence are wholly insufficient to meet the overwhelming force of youthful appetite and surrounding example. Instruction will indeed present a feeble barrier against this tide, if parents be not united in opinion and practice. *Union is the soul of parental authority, of successful education, and of domestic happiness.* The cases are extremely rare in which one parent has a right to pursue a course relative to children to which the other is conscientiously opposed. If a mother, secretly or openly, countenance her children in amusements of which their father religiously disapproves, she not only violates her sacred duty to her husband, but with her own hands demolishes the foundation of her domestic felicity. Her conduct will produce a reaction upon herself, the tremendous effects of which can be estimated by those only who have seen a mother slighted and despised by the children whom she wickedly indulged. But the child who yields a prompt obedience to the wise, firm, and *united* authority of his parents, and who is not abandoned to his own guidance by their early relinquishment of the right to control him, will ordinarily respect their opinions as he advances in years and will allow to their wishes the authority of commands.

In conclusion, I can only say during the tender concerns and frequent watchings of infancy, when discouraged by the waywardness and ever-recurring folly of childhood, and when afterward in their youth you find your mind assailed by that insidious and powerful temptation, parental ambition, strengthen your resolution, renew your courage, and repress unhallowed wishes by the oft-repeated dedication of yourself and your offspring in fervent prayer to God. Daily inquire what you can do to prepare them for usefulness here and for glory, honor, and eternal life hereafter. Cast off a slothful spirit and rouse yourself to untiring diligence by the consideration of the everlasting happiness, or the eternal misery, which awaits them in a future world.

After all your exertions for the good of your children, should your heart be wrung by seeing them become profligates, escaping from the sphere of parental influence, bursting the ties of parental tenderness and filial love, and spurning the remembrance of religious precept, abandon them not. Remember all your own ingratitude and alienation from God. Consider his patience and long-suffering with the rebellious, to which a parallel can never be found among finite beings. Follow your wandering children with deep commiseration and unceasing prayer to Him whose mercy endures for ever and who beholds and meets the returning prodigal. It may be that you will yet witness his blessing upon parental faithfulness, in restoring your children to the paths of virtue and obedience.

Yours,

Publisher's Postscript

AFTER READING the preceding letters, you will have undoubtedly noted the strong contrast between the home which the author advocates and the home which is common in our day. We live in an age in which the home frequently is marked by parental neglect and indulgence and by careless, rebellious, insolent children. Instead of the home being the place where children are nurtured and trained by parental love, example, and discipline, it is often merely a place to accumulate possessions, sleep, and sometimes eat. In pursuit of careers and affluence, many parents give up the care and education of their children to the day care center, the public and private school, and the baby sitter. So pervasive is parental neglect now that the state has intervened to provide not only general, health, and sex education, but also in many places it provides breakfast and lunch and that, even when school is not in session. Parents that have abdicated their God-appointed privilege and duty, now demand as their "right" that the government educate, feed, and, in short, raise their children. Furthermore, when it comes to entertainment and leisure, instead of parents giving themselves to their children in wholesome play or family outings, more often than not, the television and material possessions are substituted; or they are left without supervision to run with their peers.

The harmful effects of parental neglect and indulgence are at first manifested in the home. No longer is the home a place of security and warmth; much less is it a sanctuary of peace and worship. Rather it is cold and full of discord, a place to be left as soon as possible. Without much loving training, children often grow up distant from their parents and even their siblings, and when they do not get their own selfish ways, they rebel. What little spiritual and social duties are occasionally encouraged by parents, children commonly mock and resist. Then, many times in rebellion, they pursue the opposite behavior, giving themselves to promiscuity, licentiousness, drugs, and the occult.

It is wished that somehow the results of parental neglect and indulgence remained with children in the home. However, this is not the case. In only a few years the slothful youth becomes the unreliable employee; the promiscuous girl becomes the unwed mother; the rebel becomes the criminal.

Much of the blame for the deplorable state of affairs in the workplace, the church and the state may be traced to the home where parents have failed to raise and educate their children according to Christian principles. In commenting on the fifth commandment, Noah Webster remarks upon the effect which the home has upon society and the state:

No duties of men in society are more important to peace and good order than those of parents and children. Families are the origin of nations; the principles instilled into youth in families, and the habits there formed are the germs of the principles and habits of society and nations. If children are left without restraint and culture in early life, many or most of them will be rude in manners, and turbulent members of society. On the other hand, the subordination of children in families tends to favor subordination in citizens; respect for parents generates respect for rulers and laws; at the same time, it cherishes and invigorates all the kindly affections, which are essential to domestic happiness. In this command then we see the entire coincidence between the will of God and our own interest and happiness.[1]

Why are there so few courageous and principled gentlemen to fill places of leadership in our churches and our governments? Why are so many men passive and indolent as fathers, citizens, employees, and church members? Why are men so often without a clue as to what their identity is or what their calling

---

[1]Noah Webster, *The Value of the Bible and Excellence of the Christian Religion* (Durrie and Peck, 1834; Reprint, San Francisco: Foundation for American Christian Education, 1988), 72.

should be? And if they do figure this out, why is it frequently not until they are thirty or forty? Why do so many women forsake working at home to pursue careers outside the home? Why do pastors have to spend so many hours counselling about matters such as financial responsibility, courtesy, courting, and vocations? Why do children and women occupy so many places of authority? There are strong reasons to believe that these deep troubles which plague our society are evidences of God's judgment for forsaking Him and His ways — especially in our hearts and homes. Even as God abandoned the nation of Judah in her idolatrous ways and took away her means of economical, political, and spiritual support,[1] is He not judging peoples, cities, and nations in similar fashion today?[2]

We need homes where God is present and where His word governs the parents' nurture, education, and oversight of their children. We need homes where Christian education, such as espoused in the foregoing letters, is taught and modeled. We need such not only

[1] See Isaiah 2:5–9; 3:1–12.
[2] See Romans 1:18–32.

for our own tranquility and happiness as families, but also for the well-being of the church, the progress of the gospel, the welfare of the economy, and a stable and just government.

Let us cry to God that He will in wrath remember mercy and that, for the sake of His name and His covenant, He will grant His people repentance from parental neglect, indulgence and other sins. May He enable us to raise up a holy seed with holy ambitions to serve a holy God and to be salt and light in the corrupt and dark world. From the homes of His people, may God yet raise up many Daniels who, though they live in Nebuchadnezzar's kingdom, yet serve the living and true God without compromise, to the glory of God and the good of their fellow men both now and for generations to come.

Suggestions for Further Study

Abbott, John S. C. *The Mother at Home.* American Tract Society, 1833. Reprint. Sterling, Virginia: G.A.M. Publications, 1978.

Adams, Jay E. *Christian Living in the Home.* Phillipsburg, New Jersey: Presbyterian and Reformed Publishing Company, 1972.

Alexander, J. W. *Thoughts on Family-Worship.* 1847. Reprint. Part 2 in *The Family.* Harrisonburg, Virginia: Sprinkle Publications, 1981.

Baxter, Richard. "Christian Economics." Part 2 in *The Practical Works.* Vol. 1, *The Christian Directory.* 1673. Reprint. Ligonier, Pennsylvania: Soli Deo Gloria, 1990.

Chantry, Walter J. *The High Calling of Motherhood.* Edinburgh, England: The Banner of Truth Trust.

Clarkson, Margaret. *Susie's Babies: A Clear and Simple Explanation of the Everyday Miracle of Birth.* Grand Rapids, Michigan: William B. Eerdmans Publishing Company, 1992.

Dobson, James C. *The Strong-Willed Child: Birth through Adolescence.* Wheaton, Illinois: Tyndale House Publishers, Inc., 1978.

Doornenbal, Baukje and Tjitske Lemstra. *Homemaking: A Bible Study for Women at Home.* Colorado Springs, Colorado: NavPress, 1981.

Fleming, Jean. *A Mother's Heart.* Colorado Springs, Colorado: NavPress, 1982.

Hamilton, Andy. *Unity and Romance in Marriage.* Montville, New Jersey: Trinity Book Service, 1992. Audio Cassettes.

Hufstetler, James. *The Christian Man.* Montville, New Jersey: Trinity Book Service, 1991. Audio Cassette.

MacDonald, Gordon. *The Effective Father.* Wheaton, Illinois: Tyndale House Publishers, Inc., 1977.

Mack, Wayne A. *Your Family God's Way: Developing and Sustaining Relationships in the Home.* Phillipsburg, New Jersey: Presbyterian and Reformed Publishing Company, 1991.

MacArthur Jr., John. *The Family.* Chicago: Moody Press, 1982.

Martin, Albert N. *Biblical Training of Our Children.* Montville, New Jersey: Trinity Book Service. Audio Cassettes.

———. *The Effective Father.* Montville, New Jersey: Trinity Book Service. Audio Cassettes.

———. *The Christian Family.* Montville, New Jersey: Trinity Book Service. Audio Cassettes.

———. *How Not to Foul Up the Training of Your Children.* Montville, New Jersey: Trinity Book Service. Audio Cassettes.

McDearmon, George. *General Robert E. Lee: A Study in Christian Manhood.* Montville, New Jersey: Trinity Book Service. Audio Cassettes.

———. *A Study in Christian Womanhood.* Ballston Lake, New York: Ballston Lake Baptist Church. Audio Cassettes.

Nichols, Gregory G. *Molding Your Child's Character* Montville, New Jersey: Trinity Book Service. Audio Cassettes.

Palmer, B. M. *The Family*. 1876. Reprint. Harrisonburg, Virginia: Sprinkle Publications, 1981.

Ray, Bruce A. *Withhold Not Correction*. Phillipsburg, New Jersey: Presbyterian and Reformed Publishing Company, 1978.

Ryle, John C. *Duties of Parents*. William Hunt and Company, 1888. Reprint. Choteau, Montana: Christian Heritage Publisher, 1983.

The Shorter Catechism: A Baptist Version. Avinger, Texas: Simpson Publishing Company, 1991.

Sprague, William B. *Letters on Practical Subjects to a Daughter*. Reprint. Harrisonburg, Virginia: Sprinkle Publications, 1987.

———. *Letters to Young People*. 1830. Reprint. Harrisonburg, Virginia: Sprinkle Publications, 1988.

———. *Letters to Young Men*. 1845. Reprint. Harrisonburg, Virginia: Sprinkle Publications, 1988.

Waldron, Samuel E. *Catechism for Young Children.* Grand Rapids: Truth for Eternity Ministries.

Watts, Isaac, Philip Doddridge, et al. *The Family Altar: or the Duty, Benefits, and Mode of Conducting Family Worship.* Reprinted in *The Bible and the Closet.* Harrisonburg, Virginia: Sprinkle Publications, 1992.

Letters on Christian Education

Cover designed by Benjamin W. Geist
Composed by Simpson Graphics
Printed by Century Graphics

SIMPSON
PUBLISHING COMPANY

The righteous are bold as a lion - *Proverbs 28:1*